To lovers of nature

The dark depths of this small planet that we live upon contain a pulsing heart of such heat that it will melt solid rock in a matter of seconds. The results that occur when the swirling magma forces itself to the surface are awe-inspiring, even catastrophic. Mountains rise and fall, continents alter their shapes, entire towns have disappeared from sight. And when the convulsions at last die down again, the land may take centuries to recover. The rising smoke of the new, cooling earth, the hot breath of the living world beneath us, is constant evidence of the power that dwells within.

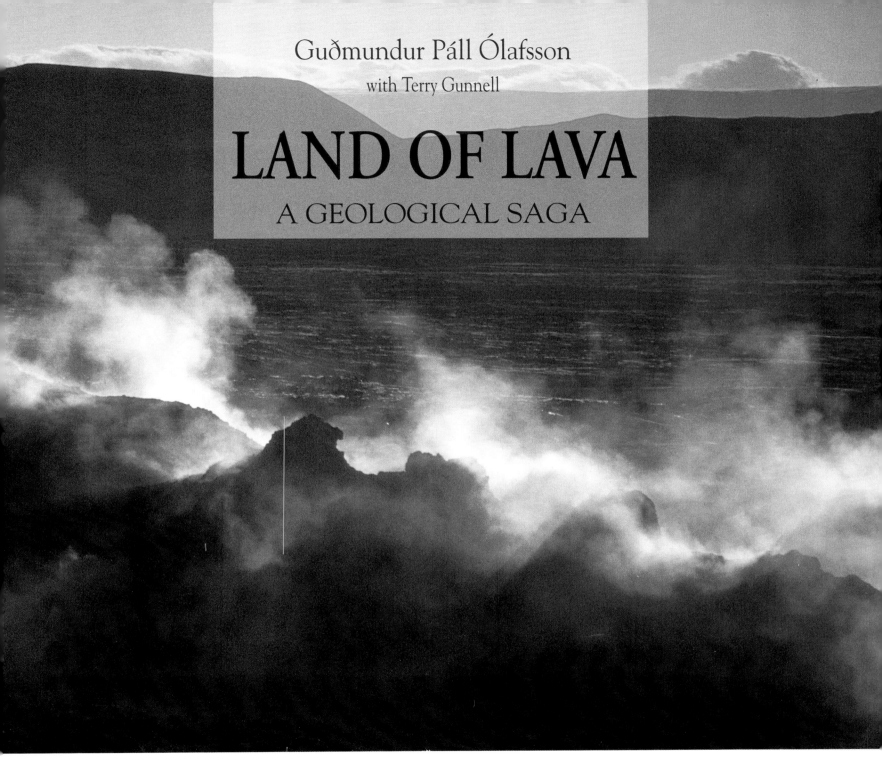

LAND OF LAVA
A GEOLOGICAL SAGA

Guðmundur Páll Ólafsson
with Terry Gunnell

Mál og menning

This isle of fire . . .

Iceland is a land of volcanoes. It is a part of the vast North-Atlantic Ridge and the only place in the world where an ocean ridge ascends above sea level. Silent, these volcanoes radiate beauty; active, they spell disaster. Their thunderous eruptions throughout the centuries form part of the history and consciousness of Icelanders. The flow of lava ruins vegetation and habitation; the gases and ashes expelled by eruptions poison the earth. They have wiped out livestock, and brought about the famine and deaths of thousands of people. Yet volcanoes also give birth to natural wonders. They have raised a land from the ocean floor.

In Dómadalur, the highlands of southern Iceland

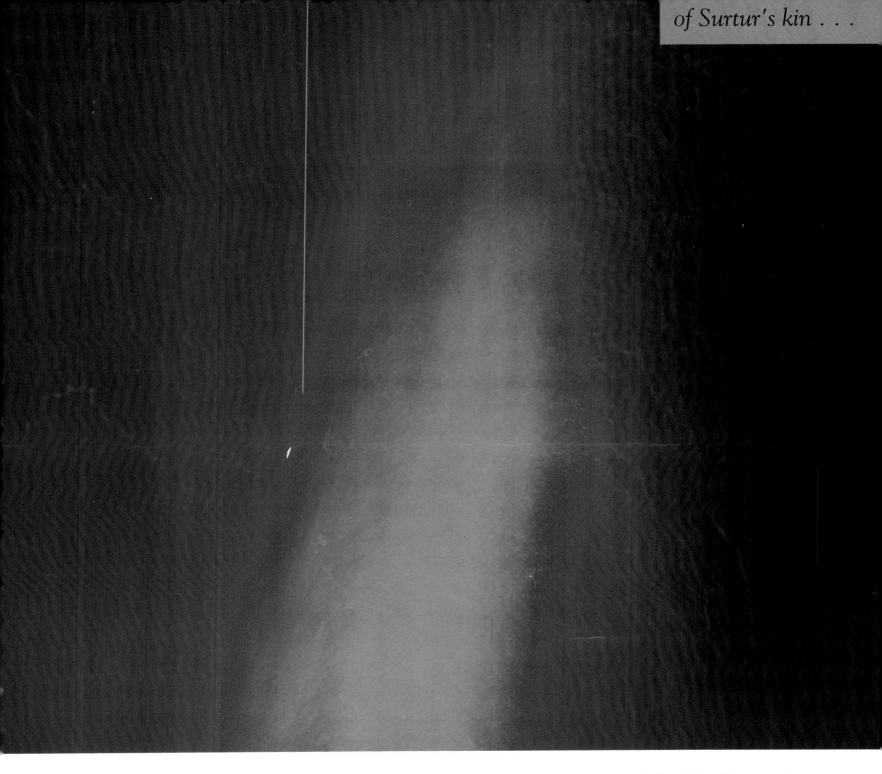

of Surtur's kin . . .

According to Nordic mythology, the gods created the earth from the body of a giant named Ymir. The vault of the sky was shaped from his skull. Ymir had many sons that drew their individual natures from the father's own personal qualities. It might be said that they represent the natural forces that clash and fight for supremacy upon the surface of this earth, inside Ymir's head. Surtur is the giant of fire and stands opposed to his brother, Ægir, who rules the sea. Their encounters beneath the turbulent Icelandic skies are frenzied, their wild furies fanned rather than cooled by their kinsman Hræsvelgur, the eagle-winged giant of the northern wind.

Volcanic eruption in Heimaey, Vestmannaeyjar

a breed marked by seas of lava . . .

Yet Ymir himself is not dead. The surface of the giant's body as it reveals itself in Iceland is marked by the gigantic forces of Ymir's conflicting characteristics. Wherever one looks, one encounters seas of tumbling lava, apparently frozen in time, the solidified life-force that once flowed from the burning heart.

Ögmundarhraun, south-west Iceland

gaping chasms . . .

In many places, the ancient surface skin of the earth has been cracked and ripped apart by numerous chasms and fissures, split by the cooling processes as the fiery life gradually departed into the air. At other times, such fissures can be the result of earthquakes, the slow death throes of the giant, the twitching of the upper reaches of Ymir's body, across which creep and clash the enormous tectonic plates known as the American and Eurasian Plates.

Flosagjá in Þingvellir, southern Iceland

and erupting geysers . . .

And the voice of the fading giant is still heard in countless variations: not merely the ear-splitting roar of the volcano, but also the more subtle gasp and splutter of the boiling mud pools, the surprising, exuberant breath of the erupting geyser brought to life by the intimate reaction of surface water meeting the burning, living earth in the turbulent volcanic regions of this unique land of ice and fire.

Strokkur in Haukadalur, southern Iceland

there is no concealing the origins ...

The hiss of the escaping steam and the scent of sulphurous odours made early foreign visitors imagine that they were approaching the gates of Hell. In actual fact, they were arriving at the scene of Creation itself, where new land was still shaping itself from the warring elements of the giant.

Kerlingarfjöll in the Icelandic highlands

the fatherhood appears in the crater . . .

About the gasping, gaping mouths of the cold craters that remain, the jagged and coagulated life-force has taken on countless different shapes in innumerable, subtle shades of colour. For the silent beholder, there can be little doubt that Surtur's fiery sword has burst out of the ground at this site, the flames of the eruption petrified for eternity.

Near Leirhnjúkur and Krafla, north-east Iceland

in the frozen strata of the lava mountains.

Elsewhere, the bare ribs of the lava mountain sides resemble a waterfall of falling, cascading waves. They have the same tale to tell as the rings of age in a severed tree stump. They mark the layers of glowing lava that flowed over this land, century after century. Today, all has been laid bare by the equally powerful forces of wind, ice and running water.

Akrafjall, western Iceland

The moment of birth: the earth rips open and utters flame . . .

The sun blackens,
earth sinks below the sea;
high in the heavens,
the bright stars are extinguished.

Flames burst forth,
from the fount of life;
the searing heat
reaches the very skies.
        Völuspá, st.57

These words from the ancient Icelandic poem, *Völuspá*, describe the end of the world at Ragnarök; the moment of death, the moment of new life, as the earth is torn apart by the pressure of the magma that eternally flows through the veins of the earth.

Volcanic eruption in Leirhnjúkur, northern Iceland

the roaring volcano bellows smoke at the heavens . . .

The fires and flames that leap from the new wound in the earth are often accompanied by shuddering earthquakes, the sound of deep thundering from beneath the ground, and billowing, heaving plumes of thick smoke that soar high into the air. The sheer enormity of the convulsions are a constant reminder of how minute and helpless humans are compared to these godlike forces.

Volcanic eruption in Heimaey, off the south coast of Iceland as the ash falls from the sky . . .

The sky, however, is not the only thing to be blackened by the eruption. These volcanic clouds lay a contaminating shroud across the once green and fertile earth, covering it with various kinds of volcanic ash, known as tephra.

Heimaey, Vestmannaeyjar, off the south coast of Iceland

the molten lava bursts free, cools, coagulates . . .

And now, from the gaping, growling mouth of the volcano, the molten life force of the giant is unleashed. The lava flows. Tongues, rivers, arms of lava roll, tumble and reach out across the stunned earth. This force is unstoppable until the wound has healed and the flames have slipped back into the darkness. The lava then commences the long process of cooling and coagulating, until it becomes solid rock.

In Surtsey, off the south coast of Iceland

and turns to stone . . .

Standing face to face with a sea of solid lava, the wanderer is easily transported into an alien, magical world that can evoke feelings of fear, excitement and wonder. The chaotic forms of the frozen lava stream play strange games with the imagination.

Frozen stream of lava near Mount Askja, in the northern highlands

in countless shapes and forms; in coils . . .

The solid sea of lava, examined at close quarters, offers an open-air gallery of natural art forms, abstract, yet mystical and symbolic. It also provides us with a concrete image of the forces that work and flow deep beneath our feet. One commonly encountered type of lava takes the form of ripples or coiled ropes. In a symbolic sense, these 'ropes' bring to mind the fetters that 'according to the Nordic myth' were supposed to bind the catastrophic force of the wolf Fenrir, brother of the serpent Jörmungandur. It was prophesied that at the time of Ragnarök the wolf would tear itself free and wreak vengeance on its captors.

Near Þorlákshöfn, southern Iceland

in pillows . . .

Another example of frozen motion is found in the so-called 'pillow lava', often created when an eruption takes place at great pressure on the ocean floor, in a lake or, sometimes, beneath a glacier. Fire meets water and creation takes place. In this case, however, the lava flows slowly, cools rapidly and forms internal columns within the 'pillows'.

Near Leirhnjúkur, north-east Iceland

and rising columns of stone.

When lava flows along the surface into a lake or a swamp, the cooling process is slower than in the ocean. However, the sudden conflict of the opposing forces makes the lava contract into large column-like units which often take a natural hexagonal shape. In some places, whole cliffs of this columnal-basalt rock can be found, a perfect example of natural architecture.

Kálfshamarsvík in Skagi, northern Iceland

The jagged aa lava is an obstacle to man . . .

There are two main types of lava fields. The so-called 'aa lava' which resembles a frozen stormy sea, can be difficult to cross. Amidst the piled, jagged lumps of clinker and slaggy debris wait innumerable pot-holes and crevices, natural traps for the careless traveller.

In Berserkjahraun, Snæfellsnes, western Iceland

bewildering, enchanting . . .

At other times, when the clouds drop from the skies and the mists start creeping down from the upper valleys, the aa lava field becomes reminiscent of the depths of the ocean floor. Size and direction become uncertain, the shadows rise, and the very surface of the land seems to alter by the minute. It is easy for a small human being to get lost in the debris of 'the giant´s wounds', a natural labyrinth.

Nýja Eldhraun, southern Iceland

a world of strange and silent shapes . . .

The aa lava fields restore to life a world nowadays confined to storybooks. As night falls, the sharp and jagged pinnacles and pillars take on new guises as faces and shapes begin to rise out of the chaotic sea of lava; people, elves, monsters, and other more fabulous creatures long lost to the eyes of humankind step forth from the darkness.

a world belonging to the hidden ones . . .

Gazing down from above, seemingly undaunted by the passing of the millennia, are the faces of the lost trolls and giants, the legendary spirits of the land itself, who once strode and fought across the face of the earth. Most of these figures have now become one with the rock that gave birth to them. Today, most of them are known only through place names.

but pahoehoe lava is of another kind . . .

The other common type of lava is known as 'pahoehoe lava'. For the most part, the wide, open seas of pahoehoe appear calm, with little more than an occasional swell to them, and very much unlike the aa lava. Indeed, the surface is often so smooth that it might have been cast in a mould.

Near Leirhnjúkur, northern Iceland

and hides another world . . .

In some places in the pahoehoe, it is possible to gain access to another world entirely, down below the ground in the hollow tunnels that once formed the subterranean passages for the magma. During an eruption, the molten lava thundered through here on on its way to the surface. When the eruption died down, the lava drained away. What remains are these silent empty caves in which icy water has sometimes taken the place of burning fire.

In Surtshellir, western Iceland

the dim world of caverns, the empty passages where lava rivers ran . . .

Farther down these caves, moving along the passageways, the wanderer in this hidden world comes upon dark forests of stone, gardens that might once have belonged to an underground kingdom.

a world of fragile stalagtites and stalagmites.

Ironically, these fragile strings of rock are the chance offspring of violent activity. When the lava drains out of the tunnels after an eruption, it is often replaced by a variety of swirling hot gases. Many of these gases are highly inflammable, and it is easy for them to ignite. When that happens the solid lava that has formed the passageways is once again brought to melting point, and starts to drip like wax. As if by enchantment, the melting lava in many caves has formed a grove of fragile stalagtites and stalagmites. It is easily destroyed.

Up above, the lava is attacked by the elements; baked by the sun . . .

Up above, in contrast to the silence down below, new rules apply. On the surface of the new earth, the lava becomes a battleground for the warring elements, the offspring of Ymir. All of these have a vital role to play in the formation of the new world that now begins to take shape as it surfaces from amidst the waves of fire. The conflicting forces of the weather are like an invisible grindstone that continuously works at the lava, smoothing its face, polishing its colour, pounding it into dust.

Rauðháls, western Iceland

soaked by the rain . . . torn by the wind . . .

*I see it rise,
a second time,
the earth out of the sea . . .*
  Völuspá, st. 59

The succeeding waves of lava, each destined to be frozen in motion, are gradually calmed, tamed and worn down by the elements through the passage of the millennia.

Near the Laki craters in the highlands of southern Iceland gnawed and ground down by the frost . . .

New lava is subjected to constant onslaught from various forces of nature. The work of ice on the new land is stupendous, and not only on the large scale. Seen up close, the detailed wonder of the natural craftsmanship involved is striking. This jewelled ice might seem fragile and short-lived, but the fragility is deceptive. Below the glittering surface, the land is being altered, ground and crushed. Water creeps into the holes, the cracks and the fissures in the lava, and then promptly turns to ice at the breath of frost. Ice is more powerful than rock, and as it grows and expands, the lava splits.

Ice crystals and frost patterns

pounded into dust by the changing weather.

Over the years, the rock constantly heats up and cools down, expands and contracts. And over time, all rock is broken down, ground into dust by the ice, the sun, the wind and the rain. Eventually it turns into soil. And once again, at the moment of apparent 'death', the spark of life is kindled. A spot of green appears.

Frost-weathered palagonite, east of Kverkfjöll, in the northern highlands

Colonisation commences with a burst of lichen . . .

Lichens, the pioneering colonists of the new lava fields, have no need for soil. They are an individual blend of fungus and one or two different species of algae. Grey and white lichens are often the first to settle amidst the inland lava of Iceland, while this yellow lichen more commonly springs up near the sea. Some lichens are like mineature self-sufficient factories that can produce nitrogen from the air. Since nitrogen must be present to enable most plants to grow, the lichens in fact help to create the necessary environment for other forms of life. The sun heralds a new dawn on the horizon of the world.

The yellow lichen (*Calaplaca verruculifera*)

mosses spread a soft blanket across the ravaged land . . .

At about the same time as the lichens start appearing, another wave of colour begins to spread across the solidified lava, removing the sharp edges, stilling the flame, calming the fury: the new rock is gently clad in a gown of moss. The soft, thick mosses, like *Racometrium lanugenosum* and *Racometrium ericoedes*, thrive in the lava where they spread widely. And once the moss has gained a hold, and the lichen starts producing nitrogen, other species of plants begin to appear.

In Nýja Eldhraun, southern Iceland

while the spider spins and searches for prey . . .

The living garb of the lava has many colours not created by plants alone. Here and there in the cracks, a jewelled and silver shimmer has been added by the most expert of weavers. The spider is one of the first hunters to settle in this new territory. As time marches on, more inhabitants move in, and the complex, exquisite threads of fate are gradually woven into the new landscape.

the lava is taking on a new life . . .

Viewed from above at different times of the year, the total effect of the new apparel created in the lava field by the combined activity of insect and plant life is striking: it represents a symphony of subtle, ever-changing colours and textures. Every square metre of the softening lava landscape provides an image of contrasting elements woven together in natural harmony.

as the swaying flora multiplies . . .

The music of creation continues to grow in volume, size, and colour. Flocks of waving ferns steadily advance through the shady crevices in the lava. Their roots take firm hold in the new soil formed by the combination of the new moss and the lava that has been pounded into dust by the action of the weather.

A garden of ferns in a lava crevice

and the bright-eyed berries bear fruit . . .

And amidst the moss and grass, tiny petals begin to open; seeds start to fly and fall, and the lava gives birth once more. Fields of berries appear in an explosion of blues and reds.

Simultaneously, the elements of taste and scent are added to the harmony of colour. Gradually, day by day, the plants are beginning to take over the surface of the lava.

In Grábrókarhraun, western Iceland

as the bushes and trees thrive . . .

As time goes by, yet further sounds fill the air with an intricate melody. Whispering bushes and swaying, rustling trees rise above the undergrowth. This was the paradise that greeted the Scandinavian and Gaelic settlers of Iceland in the ninth century.

In Borgarfjörður, western Iceland

and the butterflies flit through the air . . .

Yet none of the flowering vegetation could have appeared without help. The flowers attract insects which add their own tones to the new, faint music of the lavafield. The hovering, humming insects bear pollen, and encourage the advance of the vegetation into new territories. They are also an important source of food for other creatures, such as sparrows and their young. The colonisation continues.

The grey mountain carpet butterfly

as the eagle lays claim to a new kingdom . . .

*Falls roar,
and the eagle flies,
searching for fish,
above the mountain side.*
         Völsupá, st.59

For the sea-eagle, the lava field is a kingdom. Yet the arrival of this regal bird amidst the lava represents more than the appearance of a mere earthly monarch. The first Icelanders saw birds as having holy significance, and Óðinn himself, the supreme ancient god, was sometimes called 'Eagle-head' ('Arnhöfði').

and the wheatear lays claim to a niche.

The lava provides innumerable nesting grounds for many creatures of the air, great as well as small: the falcon, the raven, the tiny wren, and the wheatear, all have their place, all their own individual lines to sing in the growing chorus of winged voices that can be heard amongst the lava crags.

Wheatear

As the lava compacts, brooks begin to trickle . . .

Last of all, joining the combined yet gentle symphony of the wind, the leaves, the insects, and the birds, comes the fresh breath, the laughter and song of water dancing over stones, swirling amidst the mossy tussocks, heading towards the sea. The cracks and fissures in the porous lava have now been stopped with dust, gravel and mud, allowing the underground streams to rise to the surface and flow across the face of the rock.

pools and marshes appear in the ground . . .

Elsewhere, the water collects in hollows and gullies of the lava, resulting in the gradual formation of ponds, pools, lakes, and marshes. One can understand why such places were worshipped in the past. Water is the cradle of life. Its presence in the lava field encourages the development of flora, as the slender shapes of cotton grass, heath rushes, marsh arrow-grass and speedwell appear. The face of the lava changes day by day, and with the arrival of running water, greater changes are in store.

Cotton grass in marshland

the rivers slice out deep chasms . . .

The dancing brook flows into a tumbling stream; the stream in turn becomes a wild and thundering torrent that will permit no opposition to stand in its way for long. Once full-sized rivers have begun rushing across the lava fields, the changes in the landscape are destined to become ever more drastic. The roaring waters rip away loose rock and sand; bit by bit, they wear away the land, slowly but surely carving out canyons for themselves.

Fjaðrárgljúfur, southern Iceland

as the glaciers carve and press . . .

Even greater is the power of the glacier which spreads across the lava. It is personified in Nordic mythology in the shape of the ice giants that lie in wait to engulf the world. Glaciers have played one of the most influential roles in shaping the present-day face of this volcanic island. Most canyons and valleys in Iceland were initially created by rivers, and then ground into their present rounded shape by glaciers. These slow-moving waves of ice have planed down the land, scoured it and swept the debris ahead of them, even into the sea. If they themselves fail to bring the moraine to the sea, the rivers and the wind will continue the process.

Kvíárjökull, south-east Iceland

the waves smash . . .

Ægir, the angry and greedy giant of the sea, is also at war with the land. The sea is an immense force and continuously hammers at the coastline with its breakers, carving the land away bit by bit. The surging waves file into the very roots of the cliffs, digging beneath them, weakening their supports. The lifetime of any sea-cliff is limited. Meanwhile, on the beaches, the fallen rocks are steadily ground down, the swirling waters washing the remaining sand and gravel out into the sea.

Near Langibás, close to Þorlákshöfn, southern Iceland

and mould.

The sea gives and the sea takes. This rocky outpost which rises so steeply out of the ocean was once a volcano. Its name, Eldey ('Fire Island'), emphasises its origin. The sheer walls of this tiny island are continuously gnawed by the seething waves. The ledges and countless hollows in the walls, however, form ideal nesting grounds for sea birds. The last great auk was killed here in 1844, long after this unique bird had been wiped out in other countries. Today, Eldey is ruled by the gannet. However, the island will one day collapse into the sea and vanish, returning to the place of its origin.

Eldey, off Reykjanes in south-west Iceland

And so the lava became a house . . .

From the earliest of times, man has utilised his environment and used rocks and gravel as building materials. The careful erection of dry stone walls is an ancient skill, and such walls can still be found in many places in Iceland. In past centuries, field walls, pens for livestock, barns and houses were all commonly constructed from turf and rock. Today, most of these constructions are little more than ruins. They are fading back into their environment. This remaining seamen's hut stands beside the sea near Stokkseyri on the south coast of Iceland. Þuríðarbúð ('Þuríður's hut') is named after a famed female captain.

became a paved and stone-walled track . . .

Between the scattered places of habitation in Iceland, roads and paths were constructed. In earlier times the builders seem to have gone out of their way to ensure that their constructions blended with the environment. Later, when they were no longer in use, these roadways slowly become part of their surroundings. The oldest road in Iceland is probably 'Berserkjagata' ('The Berserks Road') which was cut through a lava field on the Snæfell peninsula. This road, according to Eyrbyggja Saga, was built by two quarrelsome Swedish berserks at least a thousand years ago. No modern roads are likely to endure this long.

In Berserkjahraun, western Iceland

became a source of heat for homes . . .

Icelanders have also made use of the living warmth of the new lava to heat up homesteads in the cool climate of Iceland. In many places hot water is drawn directly from the earth, and pumped into houses. On Heimaey an ingenious means of heating water was employed. Following the eruption on the island in 1973, cold water was run through the warm lava in pipes. The resulting hot water was then pumped into houses for central heating. The combination of technical knowledge and natural resources has worked wonders in Iceland. More often, however, the touch of humankind's hand on nature tends to be marked by irreparable damage.

A hot water plant on Heimaey, Vestmannaeyjar, off the south coast of Iceland

a source of purity worth preserving . . .

The lava fields of Iceland are the unspoiled offspring of nature, a wonder to the eye. Their wonder and purity, however, are easily corrupted and destroyed by the carelessness of man, by his refuse and mistreatment of the environment. Man's refuse has become a cancer on Ymir's fragile body. It need not be so.

In Kapelluhraun, near Hafnarfjörður, south-west Iceland

a natural treasure . . .

The pinnacles of lava, the offspring of fire standing amidst the solidified voice, breath and blood of Ymir, have a different quality. There is an agelessness, a combination of grace and 'sacred time', and an ever-constant reminder of the awful power down below.

Close to a Laki crater in the Icelandic highlands

a wonder to to the eye . . .

There is a belief found amongst most early peoples that deep within the earth it is possible to find the key to wisdom, the knowledge of endings and beginnings. Old Nordic mythology, for example, tells of two mysterious wells that existed beneath the roots of the world tree. One of these, Urðarbrunnur, might be seen as the Well of Fate while the other, Mímisbrunnur, was a well of wisdom.

At Þingvellir

be it at Eldborg . . .

Most of the gaping mouths that once uttered the spluttering lava are now silent. Their silence, however, is deceptive. The process of creation is everlasting. As long as Iceland continues to rest on a volcanic 'hot spot', there is always a chance that the mouths will one day find their voices again.

Eldborg in Hnappadalur, western Iceland

or Þingvellir . . .

Þingvellir is the original site of the Alþingi, the ancient Icelandic parliament and the first national parliament in the world. Nowadays preserved as a national park, Þingvellir is set in a small rift valley where the land has sunk between the two tectonic plates. Almannagjá, 'the People's Chasm', formed a powerful backdrop and natural sounding board for parliamentary proceedings. Here, one thousand years ago, the Icelandic chieftains made their momentous decision to abandon the ancient gods and adopt the God of Christianity. According to legend, the decision was greeted by a small volcanic eruption close to the site.

Almannagjá, Þingvellir

or in the dark citadels of the hidden ones.

According to folk belief, the lava fields of Iceland were populated by more than just birds and insects. Supposedly they were once inhabited by trolls, dwarves and elves. Even today, they are seen as being the homes of the 'huldufólk', the hidden people. Dimmuborgir, 'the dark citadels', near Mývatn, is a perfect example of such a site. These jagged crags and sinister rock formations that rise out of the undergrowth are a rare piece of exquisite natural art, created by the sudden draining of a lava pool that had commenced the process of solidifying.

Dimmuborgir, Mývatn, north-east Iceland

Yet all lava is destined to change . . .

The ever-changing face of the lava offers continuously new vistas, new marvels and new understanding. The feelings evoked range from terror to ecstasy, from silent awe to joyful laughter. In all cases, though, whether one is standing on the Snæfell peninsula, at the foot of Mount Hekla, or by the great row of volcanic craters at Laki, there is always a sense of that enormous power that is eternally lurking beneath the surface of the earth.

Bleikáluhraun and the Skaftá river, southern Iceland

be it in Aðaldalur . . .

The visitor to Iceland has the possibility of viewing the process of creation in a nutshell. The island is more or less composed of fields of lava that have flowed from the depths of the earth at different times over the passing centuries. Each lava field is at a different stage in the process of change. It proves that the temper of the lava can be transformed, that it will cool, change and lose its original face as the years pass by, and that it will eventually offer a home to new life, blending with the older surroundings.

In Aðaldalshraun, north-east Iceland

or Ódáðahraun.

The lava fields bear witness to the potential power that is waiting deep beneath the surface of the ground. The towering volcanoes on every horizon are merely collecting their strength. The magma is still boiling in the tunnels down below. Ragnarök has taken place, and will come again. It is part of the never-ending process of death and rebirth.

Herðubreið, in the northern highlands

It becomes grassland for grazing sheep . . .

In the meantime, humans have begun to put down roots and set up homes amidst the ancient lava flows, many of which are nowadays barely recognizable for what they are. Their edges smoothed, their surfaces ground down and blended with plant life to create a layer of soil, they have become peaceful grazing land for sheep, horses and cattle, and fertile fields for the growing of crops.

Flaga in Skaftártunga, southern Iceland

a place for children to play.

Icelandic farms used to be like living history books. The rocks in the fields and the strata exposed in the cliffs told of the volcanic activity that created the landscape. The local place names of the ancestors reflected their personal experience and understanding of their natural environment. The shapes contained within the crags and cliffs were a constant reminder of legends and the complex relationships people had with the natural spirits of the area.

Sviðnur, Breiðafjörður, western Iceland

What was once a realm of jagged lava . . .

Modern man, however, is often short-sighted and not always aware of the beauty and the fragility of the land that surrounds him. Nowadays he seldom hears the voices in the wind and rocks. As time goes on, the land often becomes little more than a resource that is used and then discarded. The unnecessary wounds that have been carved into the landscape by humankind are often deep and may never heal. Unspoiled land, however, will always be a treasure.

In Berserkjahraun, Snæfellsnes, western Iceland

of shadowy elves and trolls...

From giants	from spirits	Down from the pinnacles	whether by glaciers,
in their icy chambers,	of flame in the darkness,	the sharp eye peered,	or fingers of fire,
from elves	he learnt of his legacy,	over the homeland,	the island´s saga
in the moorland peaks,	and the fate of the land.	the open book:	was carved in stone.

Þorsteinn Gíslason:
Þorvaldur Thoroddsen

Kerling ('Old Woman') in Kerlingarfjall, Snæfellsnes, western Iceland has now become heathland . . .

*In unsown acres
crops will grow;
all ills will be cured;
and Baldur will come.*
      Völuspá, st. 62

Shaped solely by the forces of nature, the once swirling rivers of lava are transformed over time into gently sighing seas of grass and heather, rich, fertile lands of blueberry, crowberry and juniper.

Leirdalsheiði, Suður-Þingeyjarsýsla, north-east Iceland

and fields of flowers . . .

*There once more,
the wondrous pieces,
the golden chessmen,
are found in the grass,
those owned by the gods
at the gates of time.*
        Völuspá, st. 61

In Flatey, Breiðafjörður

now supports woodland . . .

Not everything fades away. Here and there, the ancient woodlands of Iceland have managed to survive. In some areas they are even thriving again. A perfect example is the forest at Hallormsstaður in the east of Iceland.

The Hallormsstaður forest, eastern Iceland

and towns . . .

It is possible for human beings to live in relative harmony with their natural surroundings. We have much to learn from our ancestors. Like them, we have the capability to create a pleasant environment in which natural and man-made architecture are combined in such a way that the origins and ancient mysticism of the land remain untouched in the present.

Hellisgerði, Hafnarfjörður, south-west Iceland

even whole cities . . .

Man continues to dominate and harness his environment, carving out a place in which to live. Reykjavík, the capital of Iceland, has been built upon ancient lava which has now largely disappeared beneath the houses, streets, gardens and parkland of the busy city. Close to Reykjavík, however, it is still possible to find clear reminders of what the site of the city once looked like. Stretches of comparatively recent lava lie just outside the suburbs of the city, and beneath this lava there is still older land.

Reykjavík, south-west Iceland

Each wave of lava has brought about an ending and a new beginning in the continuous cycle of land formation. There is no question that volcanic activity has caused Iceland great damage over the centuries. Yet it should also be kept in mind that this activity has provided the foundation of Iceland itself, and therefore the basis for existence on this northerly island. Grazing-land, vegetable garden, homesteads and even central heating in Iceland, all of these are based in one way or another upon lava, the unique force of life that was drawn from the pounding heart of the giant Ymir.

© Text: Guðmundur Páll Ólafsson and Terry Gunnell, 1997
© English translation of Völuspá and the poem page 63: Terry Gunnell
© All photographs in this book are: Guðmundur Páll Ólafsson with the exception of the following:
p 12 Axel Björnsson, p 15 Eyþór Einarsson, p 25 Sigurbergur M. Ólafsson,
p 26-27 Sigurður Sveinn Jónsson, p 49 Ingibjörg Snædal Guðmundsdóttir.

ISBN 9979-3-1395-1

Index

Aa lava 20, 21, 22
Aðaldalshraun 58
Akrafjöll 11
Algae 32
Almannagjá 55
American plate 7
Ash 4, 13, 14
Askja 16
Baldur 64
Basalt columns 19
Berries 37, 64
Berserkjagata 49
Berserkjahraun 20, 49, 62
Birds 39, 40, 41, 42, 47
Bleikáluhraun 57
Borgarfjörður 38
Breiðafjörður 61
Building with, and amidst lava 48, 60, 67, 68
Butterflies 39
Cotton grass 43
Craters 10, 54
Creation of the earth 5
Dimmuborgir 56
Dómadalur 4
Dwarves 56
Eagles 40
Earthquakes 7, 13
Eldborg 54
Eldey 47
Elves 22
Environmental damage 50, 62
Eurasian plate 7
Eyrbyggja Saga 49
Falcon 41
Fenrir 17
Ferns 36
Fjaðrárgljúfur 44
Flora 31, 32, 33, 35, 36, 37, 38, 39, 41, 64, 66
Flosagjá 7
Folk beliefs 56, 61
Forests 66
Gaelic settlers 38
Gannet 47
Gases 27
Geysers 8

Giants 23, 45; see also Hræsvelgur, Surtur, Ymir, and Ægir
Glaciers and glacial erosion, 45
Grábrókarhraun 37
Great Auk 47
Hafnarfjörður 51, 67
Hallormsstaður 66
Haukadalur 8
Heating 50, 69
Heimaey 5, 13, 14, 50
Hekla 57
Hellisgerði 67
Herðubreið 59
Hidden people: see Huldufólk
Hnappadalur 54
Hræsvelgur 5, 28
Huldufólk 23 56
Ice 30
Insects 34, 35, 39, 42
Jörmungandur 17
Kapelluhraun 51
Kálfhamarsvík 19
Kerlingafjöll 9
Krafla 10
Kverkfjöll 31
Kvíárjökull 45
Laki 29, 52, 57
Langibás, 46
Lava types 17, 18, 19, 20, 21, 24, 25
Leirdalsheiði 64
Leirhnjúkur 10, 12, 18, 24
Lichens 32, 33
Magma 2, 12
Marsh arrow-grass 43
Marshland 43
Mímisbrunnur 53
Moss 33, 36
Mud pools 8
Mývatn 56
Nitrogen 33
North Atlantic Ridge 4
Nýja Eldhraun 21, 33
Óðinn 40
Pahoehoe lava 24, 25
Pillow lava 18
Ragnarök 12, 17, 29, 40, 59, 64, 65
Rauðháls 28

Raven 41
Reykjanes 47
Reykjavík 68
Rivers and streams 44
Sea-eagle 40
Sea erosion 46, 46, 47
Settlers 38
Skaftá 57
Skaftártunga 60
Skagi 19
Snæfellsnes 20, 49, 57, 62
Sparrows 39
Speedwell 43
Spiders 34
Stalagmites 26, 27
Stalagtites 26, 27
Steam 9
Stokkseyri 48
Strata 11, 61
Strokkur 8
Subterranean passages 25
Surtsey 15
Surtshellir 25
Surtur 5, 10, 28
Sviðnur 61
Tectonic plates 7
Trolls 23, 56
Urðarbrunnur 53
Vestmannaeyjar (the Westmann Islands) 5, 13, 14, 15, 50
Volcanic activity 2, 4, 6, 8, 10, 12, 13, 14, 15, 18, 19, 25, 27, 59, 69
Völuspá 12, 29, 40, 64, 65
Weathering 11, 28, 29, 30, 31
Wells 53
Wheatear 41
Wind 11, 42
Wren 41
Ymir 5, 6, 7, 8, 15, 18, 28, 51, 69
Ægir 5, 28, 46
Þingvellir 7, 53, 55
Þorlákshöfn 17, 46
Þorsteinn Gíslason, 'Þorvaldur Thoroddsen', 63
Þuríðarbúð 48
Ögmundarhraun 6